CREATIVESCALESFOR FINGERSTYLEGUITAR

Beautiful Techniques to Create Expressive, Cascading & Dynamic Guitar Scales

WILLMcNICOL

FUNDAMENTALCHANGES

Creative Scales for Fingerstyle Guitar

Beautiful Techniques to Create Expressive, Cascading & Dynamic Guitar Scales

ISBN: 978-1-78933-463-0

Published by **www.fundamental-changes.com**

Copyright © 2025 Will McNicol

Edited by Joseph Alexander & Tim Pettingale

www.fundamental-changes.com

For over 350 free guitar lessons with videos check out:

www.fundamental-changes.com

Join our free Facebook Community of Cool Musicians

www.facebook.com/groups/fundamentalguitar

Tag us for a share on Instagram: **FundamentalChanges**

Author photo use by permission of Will Killen

Cover Image Copyright: Shutterstock

Contents

About the Author

Will McNicol is a multi-award-winning acoustic guitarist, composer, performer and tutor.

Having picked up the guitar at the age of six, Will has gone on to become *Guitarist* magazine's Acoustic Guitarist of the Year (2011), one of *Acoustic Guitar* magazine's 30 Great Guitarists Under 30 (2014), and *Guitar World's,* "one of the best acoustic players on the planet right now" (2021).

He holds Associate, Licentiate and Fellowship diplomas with Trinity College London in Classical Guitar Recital, and has released multiple critically acclaimed albums of original music.

Will has performed relentlessly throughout his career and has given concerts around the world. Whether it has been headlining his own solo shows, performing at festivals, or supporting world-renowned artists, his performances have been described as "beautifully flawless" and "magical" by the music press. Having toured, performed, and given masterclasses in the UK, Ireland, France, Germany, Italy, Canada, USA, Zimbabwe and China, Will has also taken part in concerts and workshops at one of Africa's biggest music festivals, The Harare International Festival of the Arts.

As an in-demand tutor, Will has produced educational videos for MusicRadar's Acoustic Expo and material for Imagine Publishing's Guitar for Beginners series. His compositions are proudly used throughout London College of Music's acoustic and classical guitar grade syllabuses. Will's online learning platform and community for acoustic guitarists, The College, has received critical acclaim and has welcomed hundreds of players from around the world.

Will's first book with Fundamental Changes, *Expressive Fingerstyle Guitar Techniques* was an instant Amazon bestseller and is available in Paperback, Kindle and PDF formats from **www.fundamental-changes.com**

Introduction

Scales are wonderful things! They are the building blocks that form the music we love to listen to and play. But scales are often a difficult sell in the practice room. Let's face it, it can feel uninspiring when it comes to practicing them, and especially so for fingerstyle guitarists.

My first introduction to scales was through various classical guitar syllabuses, which were filled with endless exercises to memorise. While useful for technique, the teaching material rarely explained how scales could be used in a musical way; how they could be incorporated into pieces, or creative ways to use them in order to escape their linear nature.

It wasn't until I started writing my own music, exploring the fretboard, and discovering the guitar's expressive potential that I began to see what scales were really about. Understanding them opened up my playing, deepened my understanding of the repertoire I was studying, and gave me new ways to spark creativity.

That discovery is what inspired this book.

The goal of this book is to offer you a fresh way to approach scales – one that highlights their expressive possibilities while also building your technique and fretboard knowledge.

Here's what you'll learn:

- Cascading scales using open strings that create beautiful, sustaining harmonies

- Effortless shifts between positions on the neck

- How to use dynamics, tone, and articulation to add musical expression

- Exploring harmonics to voice the notes of scales

- An understanding of how scales appear musically within fingerstyle repertoire

Each chapter will focus on a single key centre and teach dozens of exercises and examples to explore its possibilities on guitar. You'll learn practical techniques and see how they can be applied to musical examples.

At the end of the book, we'll bring everything together with some short musical studies and two complete pieces. These will show you how scale practice can transform the way you approach repertoire and open up new creative possibilities.

My hope is that by the time you finish, you'll no longer see scales as a chore, but as an exciting tool for creativity and expression. And everything you learn can be adapted to your own personal style and used to develop your voice on the guitar.

Throughout this book, you'll find fretting hand suggestions indicated by numbers above the notation, while picking hand symbols appear as letters above the TAB.

Start by practicing every example slowly, paying close attention to the suggested fingerings. These choices may not always feel intuitive but have been carefully thought through to help you achieve the best flow. As you become more confident, you can gradually increase the tempo.

If you're unfamiliar with picking hand symbols, here's a quick guide based on the Spanish terminology used in fingerstyle guitar:

- p = Pulgar (Thumb)

- i = Índice (Index or first finger)

- m = Medio (Middle or second finger)

- a = Anular (Ring or third finger)

It's also helpful to understand the concept of positions for your fretting hand. For example, first position means your first finger aligns with the 1st fret, with your other fingers naturally falling onto the 2nd, 3rd, and 4th frets. In fifth position, your first finger aligns with the 5th fret, and so on. Classical guitar notation often uses Roman numerals to indicate positions, and I've included these in key areas to highlight important shifts.

So, let's dive into a new way of looking at scales – one that puts musicality and expression at the centre of your playing!

Get the Audio

The audio files for this book are available to download for free from **www.fundamental-changes.com**. The link is in the top right-hand corner. Click "Download Audio" and choose your instrument. Select the title of this book from the menu, and complete the form to get your audio.

We recommend that you download the files directly to your computer (not to your tablet or phone) and extract them there before adding them to your media library. If you encounter any difficulty, we provide technical support within 24 hours via the contact form.

For over 350 free guitar lessons with videos check out:

www.fundamental-changes.com

Join our free Facebook Community of Cool Musicians

www.facebook.com/groups/fundamentalguitar

Tag us for a share on Instagram: **FundamentalChanges**

Get the Video

There are several supporting videos that demonstrate the more intricate techniques in this book. You can download them here:

www.fundamental-changes.com/creative-scales-bonus-videos

Chapter One: Silky Scales (E Major & E Minor)

We'll start by exploring three techniques for playing scales smoothly and beautifully. These are ideas that will immediately take you away from the mundane way of practicing scales you've probably known until now. At the heart of these ideas are what I like to call *cascading scales*. This is a way of playing scales that incorporates open strings to extend their range and adds *slurs* for fluidity.

The resulting sound of this approach can be likened to pealing church bells, where the notes ring together to create beautiful harmonies. To achieve this effect, we need to break away from standard scale shapes, build in open strings wherever possible, and find alternative positions to play the scale notes to sustain them.

Using open strings also allows us to smoothly extend the range of our scales. While an open string is ringing, we can shift our fretting hand to new positions and access other notes without interrupting the flow.

Then, adding slurs (hammer-ons, pull-offs, and slides) at key points will add a smoothness to your tone by softening the attack and reducing the workload on your picking hand.

Exploring these techniques is a fantastic way to expand your fretboard knowledge as you break out of traditional "box" shapes and discover scales in new areas of the neck. It's a great way to refine both fingerstyle and fretting techniques, as you begin to think more carefully about fingering choices to ensure consistency and fluidity.

Let's start with a cascading scale in E Major. Instead of playing the notes entirely in first position, you'll move up the neck to allow certain notes to ring together.

Pay attention to the suggested fretting fingers as they're chosen very deliberately.

The first three notes are played on the top three strings, letting the E, D#, and C# blend beautifully. Keep your first and third fingers down as long as possible, releasing your first finger only when needed to play the open B at the end of bar one.

The open B gives you time to shift position and land your second finger on the 7th fret. Through bars two and three, your first finger stays on the G# to create a sustaining harmony.

At the start of bar four, the open B allows you to shift back down the neck to complete the scale. This mirrors the opening pattern, with the top three notes blending across three strings.

Pay attention to the picking hand suggestions, as they've been chosen to ensure a smooth, flowing sound as you increase the tempo. However, feel free to experiment with your own options. Exploring alternatives is always valuable in your journey toward silky-smooth scale playing.

Example 1a: E Major – Cascading Scale

Next, let's extend the range of the E Major scale by adding another octave. The first octave remains the same as the previous example, but this time we'll continue the scale down to the sixth string.

The open fifth string at the end of bar three allows your fretting hand to shift down smoothly. It's very important to consider the position of your fretting-hand thumb throughout the examples in this book as the best way to keep your position changes smooth is by moving your thumb only *once per shift*.

Pay attention to the picking hand suggestions for this new octave: thumb, index, and middle fingers are used in a repeating pattern. Avoid using the same finger for consecutive notes, as this helps maintain fluidity at higher tempos.

As the scale moves back up, the open fifth string in bar four once again provides an opportunity to shift position while the note sustains.

Audio downloads of all these exercises are available at **www.fundamental-changes.com**. It's important that you listen to them so you can learn to match your playing to the written notation.

Example 1b: E Major – Extended Range

Now let's add slurs to the E Major scale to smooth out the attack. In the example below, hammer-ons are used on the sixth, fifth, and fourth strings as you ascend from the low E in bar four.

Ensure your hammer-ons are rhythmically and dynamically consistent. It's common for them to become rushed, or for some notes to sound weaker than others. Pay attention to the adjustments required in your picking hand technique. For example, the hammer-ons allow your thumb to pluck the starting note of each slur.

Example 1c: E Major – Adding Slurs

You'll often find these ideas used in fingerstyle pieces, so let's now apply what you've learned in a musical context. The example below adds bass notes as accompaniment while fragments of the E Major scale create a repeating melodic pattern.

In bar three, note that the 4th fret bass note is played with your first finger and requires the other scale notes to be played with an alternative fingering.

Enjoy working on the smoothness and fluidity of your playing as you explore this example.

Example 1d: E Major – Musical Context

In this second musical example, we add slurs with hammer-ons on the bass strings. While playing these hammer-ons, the open first and second strings provide accompaniment so ensure your fretting hand position allows these strings to sustain without interruption.

At the end of bar three, return to a cascading pattern with a low A acting as accompaniment. Pay close attention at the end of bar four, where a lower position of the E Major scale is used to make the repeat easier.

Use this example to refine your hammer-ons and aim for a sound that is both rhythmically and dynamically consistent.

Example 1e: E Major – Musical Context

Now that you've explored these ideas in the key of E Major, let's see how they sound with a cascading E Natural Minor scale. You'll notice that the first and last bars resemble the E Major cascading scale, with the top three notes blending across the top three strings.

In bars two and three, the open third string introduces a different picking hand pattern. Take your time to master it.

The F# and E notes in the middle bars should sustain until you shift to the 7th fret A note at the end of bar three.

Example 1f: E Minor – Cascading Scale

Let's now extend the range of this E Minor scale. As with E Major, the scale continues down beyond the initial cascade to the sixth string. This transition is made smoother by the open fourth string D note at the start of bar three.

Pay attention to the picking hand suggestions, as alternating between the index finger and thumb on the bass strings is a valuable technique to master.

Example 1g: E Minor – Extended Range

Now let's add fluidity with some slurs. This time, both hammer-ons and pull-offs are added.

The pull-offs begin in bar three, taking you down to the open A.

In bar four, transition from pull-offs to hammer-ons without plucking the sixth string again.

It's easy to accidentally sound other strings when using pull-offs if you drag across an adjacent string. Try to perform the pull-off at an angle that avoids other strings. If this proves challenging, you can flatten the finger you're pulling off to, so that it touches the adjacent string and mutes it.

Example 1h: E Minor – Adding Slurs

Let's test the skills you've learned in E Minor with a couple of musical examples.

First, this idea uses a cascading element on the treble strings to transition into a repeating *p i m* picking pattern. This pattern begins in bar three and continues through to the end of the example. Ensure the third and fourth strings ring uninterrupted, as they provide harmony for the changing bass note.

Notice how the voicing of this scale creates a bassline melody. This is one of the great advantages of exploring scales this way – it often leads to creative musical ideas you might not have otherwise discovered.

Example 1i: E Minor – Musical Context

Our next example opens with hammer-ons while the open first string acts as a subtle accompaniment. The second half makes the most of the cascading effect by moving up the scale three notes at a time. Pay attention to the picking-hand fingering suggestions as they aim to help you create fluidity throughout.

Example 1j: E Minor – Musical Context

Take your time learning the examples in this chapter and enjoy exploring the blend of cascades, extended scale ranges, and slurs. Experiment with fretting and picking hand options to create a smooth, harp-like effect, even at faster tempos. There are often many ways to subtly alter the nuance of the tone and phrasing, especially with the picking hand, so it's valuable to experiment with these from day one.

Try to create your own variations on the musical examples in this chapter.

Chapter Two: Silky Scales (A Major & A Minor)

In this chapter, we'll apply what we've learned to two new keys: A Major and A Minor. Each one brings unique opportunities and challenges and will help your understanding of scales, improve your fretboard knowledge, and refine your fingerstyle technique.

Let's start with A Major. The G# in bar one can sustain as you play the F# on the second string, and that F# can continue ringing until you need to play the open B in bar two.

The C# in bar two can sustain until you play it again in bar three. Pay attention to the D in bar three; using your fourth finger here allows the A at the beginning of the bar to sustain all the way to the end of the scale.

Example 2a: A Major – Cascading Scale

Now let's extend the range by adding another octave down to the A note on the fifth string. Pay attention to the picking hand options in this lower octave, where a combination of thumb, index, and middle fingers is used to create a smooth flow between the notes.

Shifting your third finger down one fret between bars two and three allows you to reach the 4th fret note in bar three smoothly with your first finger. The opposite movement helps you transition back up between bars five and six.

Example 2b: A Major – Extended Range

Now let's add some slurs. This example incorporates hammer-ons, pull-offs, and slides.

An initial pull-off from the second to the first finger in bar one brings smoothness to the start of the scale. The third-finger movement in the previous example is now performed as a slide. Keep the pressure on the string as you slide between the frets to ensure the destination note retains its volume.

On the way back up the scale, in bars five and six, a hammer from the 4th to the 6th fret leads directly into a slide to the 7th fret without plucking the string again. Hammer-ons into slides are an excellent technique to master as they create fluid, seamless phrases.

Example 2c: A Major – Adding Slurs

Now that you have a feel for playing the A Major scale with these techniques, let's explore it in a musical context.

Here we'll play the first octave of the cascading scale, adding slurs and a simple bass accompaniment. The piece is in 3/4 and you'll notice that by rearranging the notes of the scale, a melody emerges in the first line which is supported by sustaining open bass strings.

The second line fills the gaps left in the first. The shapes formed in this voicing of the A Major scale facilitate the arpeggiated moments seen in bars five and six.

Practice this example slowly and take time to experiment with different fretting and picking hand options. Building a strong foundation will help you achieve a silky-smooth performance when it comes to creating your own examples.

Example 2d: A Major – Musical Context

Let's return to 4/4 and explore more of the lower octave. The fourth-string slides reappear here, followed by arpeggiated patterns in the higher part of the scale. Pay attention to the fretting hand suggestions in bar two to ensure the shape you form can sustain properly.

The second line develops a repeating pattern around the bass strings. Your fourth finger frequently plays 7th fret notes, so carefully focus on its placement to avoid accidentally choking the sustain of other strings.

When using your fourth finger on the bass strings, try to be mindful of your elbow position. Bringing your elbow closer to your body allows for a more relaxed wrist rotation and makes it easier to reach across the strings. This, in turn reduces strain on your body and improves accuracy.

Example 2e: A Major – Musical Context

Now let's explore the cascading A Natural Minor scale. Bar one differs from the A Major version as the opening note can sustain until you play the open E. The middle bars are similar to the A Major version, with the notes sustaining for the same durations.

Take note of the fretting hand change at the end of bar three. As with the A Major version, switching to your fourth finger for the D allows the A at the beginning of the bar to sustain through to the end of the scale.

Example 2f: A Minor – Cascading Scale

Now let's add the lower octave into the mix.

This example introduces a larger stretch between your first and fourth fingers on the fretting hand. Use the open third string at the start of bar three to adjust your hand position in preparation for these stretches.

Staying relaxed as you move around the fretboard is essential for maintaining a smooth sound and feel. One way to achieve this is by always being prepared for the next move. Always keep your fingers close to the fretboard and hover over the notes you're about to play.

If the stretch between the 3rd and 7th frets feels too challenging right now, don't worry. It's something you can build toward. In the meantime, you can lift your finger from the fret slightly earlier to make a small hand adjustment. This will help you reach your target comfortably while ensuring the note is well-articulated.

Example 2g: A Minor – Extended Range

Adding slurs is the next step, and the example below incorporates hammer-ons and pull-offs to create more fluidity.

The first pull-off in bar one can be challenging to articulate cleanly without sounding the first string as your fourth finger moves away. To improve the accuracy of the pull-off, focus on the angle of your release and ensure the fourth finger moves up and over the first string as it leaves the string. Use the same approach at the start of bar two. This technique can be tricky, so don't worry if you occasionally graze the first string. Your accuracy will improve with slow, deliberate practice.

As you ascend the scale in the second line you'll encounter two hammer-ons that mirror the downward movement from earlier. Aim for consistency in volume and rhythm, ensuring the hammer-ons are as strong and consistent as the plucked notes.

Example 2h: A Minor – Adding Slurs

Now you're familiar with this voicing of an A Minor scale, let's play it in a more musical way.

This example introduces a dotted rhythm at the beginning. If you're unsure how this should sound, refer to the recordings for guidance. We then move into an arpeggiated pattern played by holding different notes of the scale simultaneously to form a chord shape.

The second line begins with a repetition of the first rhythm, followed by a variation of the arpeggiated pattern that adds a couple of hammer-ons. Take your time to ensure you're comfortable with your picking hand choices here, as they differ from those in the first line.

The fifth string bass creates a simple accompaniment and should sustain without interruption.

Example 2i: A Minor – Musical Context

The next example focuses on the stretch between the 3rd and 7th frets, which was discussed earlier. It is a great opportunity to practice this stretch while keeping your fretting hand relaxed.

The choice of the third finger for the 7th fret in bar two might feel counterintuitive since you've just used your fourth finger on that fret. However, this change prepares your fretting hand for the position shift needed later in bar four to voice the chord.

Alternatively, you could use the fourth and second fingers for this shape, allowing your fourth finger to handle all 7th fret notes in the example. As always, it's worth exploring different options to find what works best for you. The goal is to work towards what feels and sounds most relaxed, helping you build fluidity and consistency in an enjoyable way.

Example 2j: A Minor – Musical Context

Now that you've explored these concepts for achieving silky-smooth scale playing, you can start applying them to different tunes in your repertoire. As mentioned earlier, these techniques often appear in fingerstyle pieces, so try incorporating what you've learned into any music you're currently working on.

Create your own ideas based on the material in these first two chapters. Compose short pieces or re-voice scales you already know to include cascades. Both exercises will reinforce what you've learned while deepening your fretboard knowledge.

If you've been enjoying the cascading scales in these chapters, you can look forward to the bonus chapter at the end of the book, where I've included even more for you to explore.

Chapter Three: Rich Scales (G Major & G Minor)

Being able to add musical expression into your scale playing is a helpful skill to develop, as it can be transferred into every aspect of your guitar playing.

In the next two chapters, you'll learn how to play scales with a variety of *dynamics*, *tone*, and *articulation*, and discover how these elements combine to great effect when placed in musical context.

Dynamic variety simply means playing notes at different volumes. Being able to confidently play scales from as quiet as a whisper to as loud as a shout will give you great control over your technique, and adding dynamic contrast to your playing is an excellent tool to have when it comes to communicating musical expression.

Here are the dynamic terms you'll encounter over the next two chapters:

- ***p*** = *piano* = quiet

- ***mp*** = *mezzo piano* = moderately quiet

- ***mf*** = *mezzo forte* = moderately loud

- ***f*** = *forte* = loud

- $<$ = *crescendo* = gradually getting louder

- $>$ = *diminuendo* = gradually getting softer

Tonal variety is created by shifting your picking hand between the three main tonal areas of the guitar: near the neck, near the bridge, and halfway between the two. Classical guitarists use specific terminology for these techniques:

- ***dolce*** = *sweet* (picking hand near the neck)

- ***naturale*** *(nat.)* = *natural* (picking hand halfway between neck and bridge)

- ***ponticello*** *(pont.)* = *bridge* (picking hand by the bridge)

Articulation refers to how you shape individual notes. In this chapter, we'll focus on three key articulations:

- ***Staccato***: A small dot above or below the notehead, indicating you should cut the note short

- ***Tenuto***: A small straight line above or below the notehead, telling you to hold the note for its full length

- ***Accents***: Small wedge symbols above or below the notehead, indicating the note should be played more forcefully

We'll begin with the two-octave G Major scale shape shown below. The "p" markings indicate all notes should be played with your thumb.

When using your thumb exclusively, rest your index, middle, and ring fingers on the first string to stabilise your hand, while keeping the fingers ready for use. When your thumb moves to play notes on the first string, lift these fingers slightly, then return them to their resting position for notes on other strings.

To ensure your fretting hand can comfortably span the required frets, practice keeping each finger down as you ascend the scale. For example, at the start of the scale, play the first note, G, with your second finger, keeping it down as you add your fourth finger to the 5th fret. Reset when you move to the next string and repeat this approach. This helps train your fretting hand to stay efficient, minimising unnecessary movement while maintaining an optimal position.

Example 3a: G Major Scale Shape

Now explore some simple dynamic variety. Play the ascending half of the scale *forte* before dropping to *piano* as the scale descends. Ensure that you can hear the difference in dynamics, as *forte* and *piano* are at opposite ends of the dynamic spectrum.

Pay attention to how your thumb feels as you shift between dynamics, and make sure you maintain rhythmic stability and accuracy throughout.

Start slowly, to get comfortable with the changes, then gradually increase the tempo as you build confidence.

Example 3b: G Major – Dynamic Variety

Accents adds dynamic variety through articulation. I like to think of them as micro-dynamics, as they cause you to play specific notes with extra power.

Alternating quickly between accented and normal notes is a valuable skill, and the example below is designed to help you develop it. Every other note in the scale is marked with an accent. Practice moving between strong and normal dynamics in a repeating pattern.

Again, ensure this focus on articulation detail doesn't affect the overall flow of the scale. If it does, slow down your playing and gradually increase the tempo as you regain control.

Example 3c: G Major – Accents

The final element of musicality we'll explore is the use of *staccato* and *tenuto*.

The ascending part of the scale should be played *tenuto*, indicated by small lines above or below the noteheads. This means you must hold each note for its full duration before moving on. You might think you're already doing this, but it's common for notes to end early as you anticipate the next one. Focus on holding the *tenuto* notes as long as possible before moving to the next.

The descending half of the scale should be played *staccato*, marked by dots above or below the noteheads. *Staccato* notes are much shorter in duration, and you can create this effect in two ways:

1. Quickly release the pressure from your fretting-hand finger to stop the note from sounding. Be careful not to lift your finger completely off the string, as this can create an unintended pull-off.

2. Use your picking-hand thumb to mute the string immediately after playing it. This method adds an extra motion for your thumb, so if it's new to you, start slowly and build accuracy over time.

Use the example below to practice both techniques.

Example 3d: G Major – Staccato & Tenuto

Now that you've played through the G Major scale and explored various musical options, let's try some melodic ideas using this shape. Use your picking-hand thumb to continue developing its control.

Our first melody combines dynamics with *forte* for the first line and *piano* for the second, where the melody descends the octave. It also features accents in a repeating two-bar pattern. The first bar places an accent on the off-beat of beat 2, while the second bar accents beats 1 and 3.

Before adding dynamics and articulations, ensure you can play the melody confidently without them. Practice slowly and listen to the recording to familiarise yourself with the rhythms. When you're ready, focus on making the accents noticeably more powerful than the other notes and creating a clear distinction between the *forte* and *piano* dynamics.

Example 3e: G Major – Musical Context

Our next musical example features more frequent dynamic changes along with *staccato* and *tenuto*.

The first two-bar phrase should be played *tenuto* with a *forte* dynamic. This is followed by a *staccato* and *piano* phrase. The second line follows a similar pattern, where the first two-bar phrase is *tenuto* and *forte*, then transitions to *staccato* and *piano*.

For the *tenuto* notes, ensure they sustain for their full duration before moving to the next note. In stark contrast, the *staccato* notes should be cut short using one of the methods discussed earlier.

Example 3f: G Major – Musical Context

Let's move on to G Minor. The example below introduces a transpositional G Natural Minor scale shape with the root on the sixth string. This scale is slightly more challenging due to the position change on the third string, which occurs in bar three and bar five. Take time to practice this position change, and use the Roman numerals as a guide to remind you where the shifts occur.

As before, anchor your fingers on the first string while using your thumb to pick throughout. When playing the final note on the first string, lift your fingers briefly, then return them to the first string for the remainder of the scale.

Example 3g: G Minor – Scale Shape

Earlier in this chapter you explored *forte* and *piano* dynamics. Now let's expand this to include *mezzo-forte* (*mf*), which means moderately loud, and *mezzo-piano* (*mp*), which means moderately quiet. Developing a full range of dynamics will help to make your playing much more expressive.

In the example below, each octave of the G Minor scale is played with a different dynamic. Start at *forte* until you reach the middle G at the end of bar two, where you drop to *mezzo-forte*. At the top of the scale, drop further to *mezzo-piano*, and finally, return to *piano* on the middle G.

Ensure these dynamic changes are noticeable while maintaining an overall balance throughout your playing. Avoid dropping too far in volume with each step, as you'll run out of room to play quieter. Likewise, make your *forte* loud enough to provide space for the gradual decrease in dynamics.

Example 3h: G Minor – Dynamic Variety

Another element when shaping the musicality of your scale playing is tonal variety. The G Minor example below moves between the three main tonal areas of *ponticello* (*pont.*), *naturale* (*nat.*), and *dolce*.

Start with your picking hand near the bridge to play the *ponticello*. When you reach the middle G at the end of bar two, move closer to the sound hole to create the *naturale* tone. Then, as you reach the top G of the scale, shift your hand near to the neck to play *dolce*. The descending half of the scale works in reverse, finishing back at *ponticello* for the final note.

Teaching your picking hand to move confidently between these regions while staying relaxed is important as the tone of your playing affects every note you perform.

If this picking hand movement is new, you might find it harder to play accurately in the *ponticello* and *dolce* areas. Anchoring your fingers on the first string while playing with your thumb can act as a helpful guide as you transition between the three positions.

Practice this slowly and enjoy the different sounds these tonal areas produce. The tonal spectrum of the acoustic guitar is vast and is one of the most effective tools for creating musical variety in your playing.

Example 3i: G Minor – Tone Variety

Before we move on to exploring musical context, I want us to look at one further element that will add expression to our playing: the use of rest stroke (*apoyando*) and free stroke (*tirando*). These are the two main playing techniques used by classical guitarists and being able to switch between the two depending on the musical context is a valuable skill to have, as it creates a rich texture in your playing.

If these terms are new to you, rest stroke means that the plucking finger rests on an adjacent string after playing its note. With free stroke, the note is played, then the fingers or thumb move freely towards the hand. The striking finger (or thumb) does not touch an adjacent string.

When playing *apoyando*, pluck confidently downward with your thumb, allowing it to come to rest on the string below immediately after the pluck. This technique produces a powerful sound and allows for louder dynamics than *tirando*.

When playing tirando, adjust your hand position to enable a smooth motion of your thumb *through* the plucked string and out and away from the other strings.

Example 3j: G Minor – Rest Stroke & Free Stroke

Let's play what you've learned in a more musical context.

This melody combines the *tirando* and *apoyando* techniques with tonal variety. Play the first half of the scale *tirando*, with your thumb plucking through and away from the strings. When you reach the second line, where the melody moves to the bass strings, switch to *apoyando*, plucking down and resting your thumb on the string below.

Tonal contrast is created by changing hand position every two bars. Start *dolce*, with your picking hand near the neck for the first two bars. In bar three, move to *naturale* (*nat.*), in the central position. The second line takes your hand down to the bridge for *ponticello*, before returning to *naturale* for the final two bars.

Before adding these techniques, build confidence by playing the melody first, then add the musical elements one at a time before combining them.

Example 3k: G Minor – Musical Context

Now let's combine dynamic and tonal contrast.

The first two bars should be played *piano* (*p*), followed by a shift to *mezzo piano* (*mp*). In the second line, move to *mezzo forte* (*mf*), and finish the last two bars at *forte* (*f*).

Once you're comfortable with the dynamic changes, add the tonal contrast. In the first line, transition from *dolce* to *naturale*. The final line should be played entirely *ponticello*.

Take your time exploring how these techniques enhance the sound of your guitar. Add them into your current repertoire, and use them to develop your own ideas.

Example 3l: G Minor – Musical Context

The scales we explored in this chapter used transpositional shapes. In other words, they didn't involve open strings. This means you can move them up and down the neck to play in different keys. Try playing them in different areas of the neck to discover how they sound and feel in different locations.

Chapter Four: Rich Scales (C Major & C Minor)

In this chapter, we'll explore two more transpositional scale shapes in C Major and C Natural Minor with roots on the fifth string.

We'll also shift the focus to playing with your picking-hand fingers rather than the thumb, and use a walking pattern between the index and middle fingers. Being proficient with both techniques provides essential flexibility and allows you to adapt, depending on the musical context.

When picking a melody with your fingers, rest your thumb on the sixth string for stability.

Begin by learning the two-octave C Major scale shape shown below.

Pay attention to the position change from the 2nd to 5th fret at the end of bar two and practice it until your fretting hand moves smoothly and stays relaxed. The opposite shift happens in bar six as you descend back to 2nd position.

It's worth practicing this slowly, as it always feels different on the way back down.

Example 4a: C Major Scale Shape

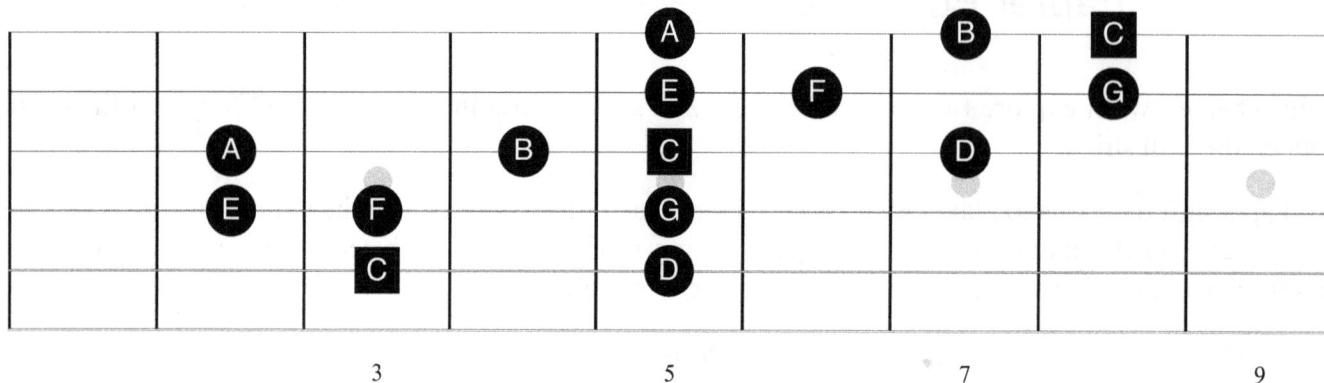

Now you've mastered the basic shape, let's explore dynamic contrast in a new way.

Previously, you worked on stepwise dynamic changes, moving between *piano*, *mezzo piano*, *mezzo forte*, and *forte*. This time, we'll focus on smoothly increasing and decreasing dynamics using *crescendo* and *diminuendo*. This approach will also help your picking-hand fingers learn to transition between different dynamic levels.

Begin the scale at *mezzo piano* (*mp*) and gradually build to a peak of *mezzo forte* (*mf*) by bar four. The key to a confident crescendo is to avoid reaching the loudest point too quickly. Aim for a gradual swell.

After reaching the peak of *mezzo forte* (*mf*) in bar four, reverse the process with a *diminuendo* back down to *mezzo piano* (*mp*) to finish the scale.

Example 4b: C Major – Dynamic Variety

Let's add accents with your picking-hand fingers. In the example below, you'll see an alternating pattern of accents across each octave.

In bar one, accent the first and last notes, playing them louder than the others. In bar two, only the second note should be accented. This pattern continues throughout the scale.

Accents can create engaging rhythmic features by emphasising less obvious beats. Take your time with this example, ensuring that every accent sounds noticeably stronger than the surrounding notes.

Example 4c: C Major – Accents

Now let's practice *staccato* and *tenuto* using your picking-hand fingers.

In the example, the ascending half of the scale should be played *staccato*, with notes intentionally cut short. The descending half should be played *tenuto*, allowing each note to sustain fully before transitioning to the next.

When using your picking-hand fingers to play melodies, it's common to inadvertently cut a note short by resting the next finger on the string too early. Take care to avoid this when playing *tenuto*, ensuring that each note sustains fully without interruption.

Example 4d: C Major – Staccato & Tenuto

Let's apply these picked expressive techniques to a melody in C Major and see how they work in a musical context.

The example below combines *crescendo* and *diminuendo* with accents. In the first line, a *crescendo* builds from *mezzo piano* (*mp*) to *mezzo forte* (*mf*). The second line reverses this, gradually returning to *mezzo piano* (*mp*) with a *diminuendo*.

As always, begin by mastering the melody without articulation and dynamics. Listen to the recording to ensure that the rhythms are accurate. Once you're comfortable, start applying the elements of musicality.

Example 4e: C Major – Musical Context

The next example combines *staccato* and *tenuto* with varying lengths of *diminuendo* and *crescendo*.

In bar one, play the notes *tenuto* at a *mezzo forte* dynamic. A short, one-bar *diminuendo* brings the dynamic down to *mezzo piano* in bar three, where the notes should be played *staccato*.

The second line features a repeating melodic pattern that gradually grows louder through a *crescendo*, culminating in a return to *mezzo forte* at the end.

Example 4f: C Major – Musical Context

The C Natural Minor scale shape will challenge your smooth position changes, as it includes three shifts.

Begin in third position and move to the fifth position at the end of bar two. There's a further shift up to the sixth position at the start of bar four.

On the way back down, the opposite shifts occur in bars five and seven. Work through these transitions slowly, ensuring you can play them confidently before moving on.

Example 4g: C Minor Scale Shape

Once you're confident, add some dramatic leaps with your dynamics. The example below explores the C Minor scale with alternating dynamics between *piano* (*p*) and *forte* (*f*) for each octave.

The key here is to maintain picking-hand accuracy as you navigate these extreme dynamic shifts. Higher volumes can often lead to a loss of precision, while quieter volumes may cause some notes to drop out.

Example 4h: C Minor – Dynamic Variety

Up to now, we've practiced moving between tonal areas in a stepwise fashion, jumping between *dolce*, *naturale* (*nat.*), and *ponticello* (*pont.*). Now let's explore a more gradual transition between these regions by moving your picking hand continuously as you play.

The dashed arrow indicates a gradual shift between *ponticello* and *dolce*. Begin the scale with your picking hand near the bridge (*ponticello*) and, as you play, gradually move toward the neck. By the time you reach the top note at the end of the first line your picking hand should be at its closest to the neck (*dolce*). On the way back down, reverse the process and gradually shift your picking hand back to the bridge so that you finish at *ponticello*.

This exercise offers two challenges:

1) Moving your picking hand while picking can introduce inaccuracy in your playing.

2) It's easy to accidentally move too quickly or too slowly between tonal regions.

As always, slow and focused practice will help here.

Example 4i: C Minor – Tone Variety

In the previous chapter, you explored *apoyando* (rest stroke) and *tirando* (free stroke) with your picking-hand thumb. Now it's time to practice these techniques with your picking-hand fingers.

It's likely that your default way of playing with your fingers is *tirando*, as it's very common in fingerstyle music. *Apoyando* may feel less familiar, so this exercise offers a great opportunity to develop the skill.

To play *apoyando* with your fingers, pluck in a downward motion and keep the finger straight so that it comes to rest on the string below. The next finger then plays the next note in the same manner.

In the scale below, start by plucking the first note of C on the fifth string with your middle finger. The finger should pluck through the string and come to rest on the sixth string. Your index finger then plays the next note, and comes to rest on the sixth string too.

At the end of the first line, switch to *tirando* by plucking up and away from the string.

Example 4j: C Minor – Rest Stroke & Free Stroke

We'll end this chapter with some melodic examples using the C Natural Minor scale.

The first example combines dramatic dynamic leaps between *forte* and *piano* with transitions between *apoyando* and *tirando*. If you're unsure how to play the rhythms, refer to the recordings for guidance.

First, learn the melody without any articulation or dynamics. Focus on the position changes, paying close attention to the Roman numerals above the notation to help you navigate them smoothly.

Example 4k: C Minor – Musical Example

This melodic example focuses on playing the melody while creating smooth movements between *dolce*, *ponticello* (*pont.*), and back.

Begin with your picking hand near the neck for *dolce*, then gradually move toward *ponticello* as you play through the first line. By the end of the first line, your picking hand should be as close to the bridge as is comfortable.

In the second line, reverse this process by gradually moving your picking hand back toward the neck to finish in *dolce* as you prepare for the repeat.

Example 4l: C Minor – Musical Example

The scales in this chapter are again transpositional shapes, so you can move them up and down the neck to play in different keys.

Chapter Five: Using Harmonics (D Major & D Minor)

In this chapter we're going to learn how to play scales using harmonics. This technique can add wonderful colour to your playing, and is one worth mastering as it increasingly occurs in all styles of acoustic guitar playing.

This chapter covers three types of harmonics: Natural, Artificial, and Harp.

Natural Harmonics

Natural harmonics are created by lightly touching a string with a fretting-hand finger directly over the fret wire of the desired fret, then plucking the note with your picking hand. They are indicated in the score by diamond noteheads, along with diamond symbols around the TAB, and the abbreviation "N.H." beneath the TAB.

The most common natural harmonics are found at the 12th, 7th, and 5th frets, but others (like those on the 9th fret) are also available.

Artificial Harmonics

Artificial harmonics are generated entirely by your picking hand. They allow harmonics to be played on fretted notes as well as open strings. To perform them, lightly touch the string with your picking-hand index finger over the metal of the desired fret, then pluck the string behind your finger with your picking-hand thumb. The diagram below shows the proper positioning of the index finger and thumb.

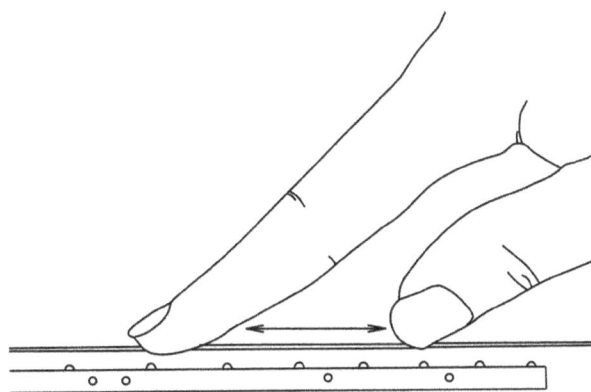

Artificial harmonics are shown in TAB with the abbreviation "A.H." beneath the number, followed by the fret where the harmonic should be touched.

For example, a 14th fret artificial harmonic would have a TAB number of "2" (indicating that your fretting hand finger is holding down the 2nd fret) with a diamond around it. Beneath the TAB will be written "A.H.14" (indicating that the artificial harmonic will be plucked at the 14th fret, 12 frets above the fretted note).

Harp Harmonics

Harp harmonics are created by alternating between artificial harmonics and normal notes, played in a repeating pattern. The artificial harmonic is played as described above, and the "normal" note is typically plucked with the picking hand's middle or ring finger. (I prefer using the ring finger, as it provides greater separation between the normal note and the harmonic, offering a clearer, more balanced sound).

We'll begin by playing a D Major scale with natural harmonics. A unique challenge with natural harmonics is that, depending on the key, you may not have all the notes needed for a complete scale. This creates interesting creative possibilities as you pick and choose from available notes or shift octaves to find the desired sound.

In the example below, we'll explore different octaves to complete a D Major scale. For instance, in bar two, jumping down an octave allows us to access the additional notes needed to complete the scale.

Tips for Playing Natural Harmonics:

Positioning: Place your fretting-hand finger directly over the metal of the fret bar.

Release Timing: Release your finger from the string *after* plucking. Avoid releasing simultaneously with the pluck, as this increases the chance of missing the harmonic. Pluck first, release afterwards.

Plucking Strength: Don't be afraid to pluck with power. Although harmonics are often associated with delicate sounds, playing them with a strong attack produces a fuller, more resonant tone, so don't hold back!

Example 5a: D Major – Natural Harmonics

One of the joys of playing scales with harmonics is how it encourages us to explore the fretboard and unlock its full potential.

Here you'll see a new voicing of the D Major scale that allows it to be played using artificial harmonics.

Begin by learning the scale without the harmonics. Ignore the diamonds on the TAB and play the notes as you would normally. You'll hear a straightforward, one-octave D Major scale in open position.

Once you're comfortable with the scale, begin applying the artificial harmonics one note at a time. Take your time adjusting your picking-hand position as you move between the harmonic positions. These positions are indicated beneath the TAB in the abbreviations.

For example, the second note in this scale requires your fretting hand to play the 2nd fret while your picking hand plucks an artificial harmonic at the 14th fret.

Example 5b: D Major – Artificial Harmonics

Once you're confident with the previous example you can move on to harp harmonics. The example below is a variation of the D Major scale you just learned. Again, begin by playing the example without harmonics to get a feel for the fretting hand movements. When that's solid, you can introduce the harmonics.

In this example, the harp harmonic effect is created by a repeated 3rd fret drone on the note D. Start slowly, as it may take time to adapt to the repeating harp harmonic pattern.

Example 5c: D Major – Harp Harmonics

To conclude our exploration of harmonics in D Major, let's use the techniques you've learned in a more musical way.

In this 3/4 example, you'll play two natural harmonics simultaneously at the beginning of bars one and three, to create a beautiful sustaining harmony. Focus on letting these harmonics ring for as long as possible by avoiding accidental contact with the strings.

The goal is to create a lush, flowing sound, allowing the harmonics to enhance the musical expression.

Example 5d: D Major – Musical Context

Next, let's combine artificial and harp harmonics.

The first two bars contain a simple melody drawn from the artificial harmonics scale you learned earlier. The final two bars add a harp harmonic pattern to that melody and combine with plucked notes on the first and second strings.

Focus on how your picking-hand ring finger moves between the strings when playing the "normal" notes in this pattern. Smooth and controlled transitions are the key to creating a balanced and expressive tone.

Example 5e: D Major – Musical Context

Now let's explore how we can play all the notes of a D Minor scale using harmonics. Unlike D Major, D Minor doesn't allow all the necessary notes to be played with natural harmonics alone, so we need to combine natural and artificial harmonics straight away.

Combining these techniques can feel challenging at first, as it involves focusing on both hands simultaneously. Learn this scale very slowly, focusing on just one note at a time. Pay close attention to which harmonics are natural and which are artificial.

Pay special attention to the transition between natural and artificial harmonics with your picking hand. The smoother and more relaxed this motion becomes, the better your sound will be.

Example 5f: D Minor – Finding All the Notes with Natural and Artificial Harmonics

Moving on, this D Minor scale is played entirely with artificial harmonics.

Start by playing the scale without harmonics to familiarise yourself with the fretting-hand movements. Once you're comfortable, you can add the artificial harmonics.

The more stable and consistent your picking hand shape is, the more reliable and steady your artificial harmonics will sound.

Example 5g: D Minor – Artificial Harmonics

This variation adds some harp harmonics with a repeating D note creating the harp harmonic element.

Again, start by playing the example without harmonics to allow your fretting hand to become comfortable with its movements. Once you've mastered this, introduce the harp harmonics for the full musical effect.

Example 5h: D Minor – Harp Harmonics

This example uses natural harmonics and creates harmony by playing two harmonics simultaneously.

Here's a timely reminder of some key tips for achieving a great harmonic sound:

- **Check your fretting-hand placement:** Ensure your finger is positioned directly over the metal of the fret

- **Don't rush the release:** Let the string ring fully by releasing your fretting finger gently after plucking

- **Pluck with confidence:** A strong, deliberate pluck gives your harmonics a lush, full sound

Example 5i: D Minor – Musical Example

Finally, let's explore D Minor using artificial and harp harmonics.

The first two bars contain a simple melody, and the second two add a harp harmonic pattern around the melody.

Don't rush! With harmonics, smooth communication between your fretting and picking hands is essential.

Enjoy the process of gradually increasing the tempo at a pace that feels comfortable and controlled.

Example 5j: D Minor – Musical Example

Chapter Six: Combining Ideas

In this chapter, we'll combine everything you've learned so far into a series of short musical examples to demonstrate how the techniques and concepts introduced earlier can come together to create expressive, musically-rich pieces.

The examples show how ideas explored in specific keys can be adapted to different areas of the neck, and real musical contexts. This will give you further insight into the fact that scales aren't just passive devices, designed to be played up and down – they're inspiring tools with which we can create beautiful music.

Our first example is in the key of E Major. You'll notice elements of cascading scales along with portions of the transpositional shapes introduced in Chapter Four. These transitions between fretboard positions are made smooth by playing open strings before each jump.

Notice the hammer-ons and the pull-off in bar three. Ensure they sound consistent and aren't rushed.

Once you're comfortable with the basic mechanics of the example, add the *staccato* in bars three, four, and five, marked with dots above or below the noteheads in the notation. These are easily missed, so read carefully!

Example 6a: E Major – Cascades, Slurs, Position Jumps, and Staccato

Next, we move to E Minor for an idea that combines natural harmonics with slower cascades.

Spend time getting to know how your fretting hand needs to move between the harmonics in bars one and three, and the slow cascades in bars two and four.

For the cascades to be effective the notes should blend seamlessly. Keep your first and fourth fingers held for as long as possible in those bars to create the harmonies.

Example 6b: E Minor – Natural Harmonics and Cascades

Let's move to A Major for an example that combines *dolce* and *ponticello* with cascades and slurs. In this example, the cascading scale idea has been adapted to form a melody using selected scale notes.

Start by learning the example without any tonal variety to give your fretting hand the chance to get comfortable with the other aspects of the piece. Once you feel confident, begin incorporating the movement of your picking hand between the neck (*dolce*) and the bridge (*ponticello*).

Example 6c: A Major – Tonal Variety, Cascades, and Slurs

Up to now, the examples have required your picking-hand thumb to add bass notes as accompaniment. Now, we'll use the thumb to articulate a melody before moving back to playing with your fingers.

The first half of the example should be played entirely *apoyando* with your thumb. In the second half, switch to *tirando* and use your picking-hand fingers. Developing the ability to confidently alternate between these picking-hand techniques is an important skill for expressive performance.

A final element to consider in this example is how to move your fretting hand efficiently between positions. You need to anticipate the position shifts and prepare for them in advance to avoid hesitation during your performance.

Example 6d: A Minor – Rest & Free Stroke with Smooth Position Shifts

Let's move to G Major to work on a four-bar *diminuendo* while navigating position shifts. There's a natural harmonic added at the end for good measure!

Begin without the dynamic layer to learn the mechanics and give your picking and fretting hands the chance to get comfortable with the basic notes and movements. Once you're confident, introduce the gradual *diminuendo*, moving from *mezzo forte* to *piano* over the four bars. Don't rush the decrease in volume, and try to create a smooth, controlled dynamic change.

Example 6e: G Major – Dynamics, Slurs, Position Shifts, and a Natural Harmonic

Moving to G Minor, we'll combine tonal variety with *staccato*, *tenuto*, and accents. Notice the *staccato* moments on beat 2 of bars one and three. These notes must be short and precise.

Beat 3 combines *tenuto* with an accent, so as well as holding these notes for their full duration, you must play them more forcefully than the others.

Once you've incorporated these articulation elements, turn your attention to tonal variety. Play the first two bars *ponticello* and switch to *naturale* for the final two bars.

Example 6f: G Minor – Tonal Variety and Articulation

This C Major example combines hammer-ons with *crescendo* and *diminuendo*. The first part of the scale recalls the transpositional shapes you learned earlier and uses the open first string to allow space for a smooth transition into open position.

Focus on making your hammer-ons smooth and deliberate. Once the hammer-ons feel consistent, add the one-bar *diminuendo* at the beginning of the example and a *crescendo* at the end. Maintaining control of your picking hand is essential when articulating these dynamic shifts.

Example 6g: C Major – Dynamics, Slurs, and Smooth Position Shifts

Moving to C Minor, this example focuses on *apoyando* with your thumb. The melody's notes are all from the transpositional shapes covered earlier in the book.

Once you've mastered the basic playing, add the dynamic shift from *forte* to *piano* found in the middle of the example.

Finally, add some tonal variety. Begin playing *ponticello* for a bright tone, then transition to the sweeter sounds of *dolce* as the idea progresses.

Example 6h: C Minor – Rest Stroke, Dynamics, and Tone

Here's a D Major idea that combines artificial harmonics with slurred scale ideas drawn from the transpositional shapes you've practiced.

It begins with a short melody played using artificial harmonics. Learn the transitions of your picking hand slowly to ensure the harmonics are voiced cleanly.

Move to 7th position to play a melody that incorporates pull-offs. The open first string at the end of this section provides a moment to reposition your hands and prepare for a repeat of the artificial harmonics.

It concludes with another short melody in 7th position, this time with a pull-off and a hammer-on articulation.

Example 6i: D Major – Artificial Harmonics and Slurs

To round off this chapter, let's move to D Minor for this 6/8 example. It includes notes from the transpositional shapes you've learned, along with cascading moments, an extended *diminuendo*, and a short *crescendo*.

In the middle of bar four, the open string allows for a smooth transition from 7th to 5th position. For the return to 7th position at the end of the example, slide your second finger from the 6th to the 8th fret.

Once you've mastered the position changes, add the three-bar *diminuendo* from *forte* to *piano*. Ensure the dynamic change is gradual and avoid reducing the volume too quickly. Finally, incorporate the short *crescendo* in the final bar, building from *piano* back to *forte* to prepare for the repeat.

Example 6j: D Minor – Dynamics, Cascades, and Position Shifts

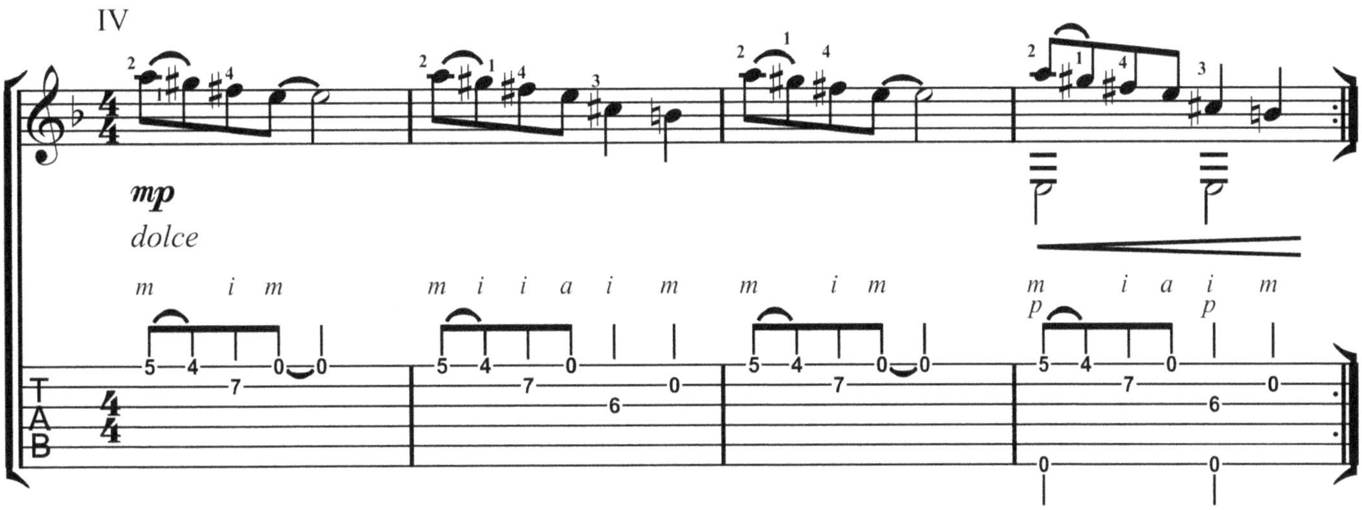
IV
mp
dolce
m i m
m i i a i m
m i m
m i a i m
p p
TAB

Chapter Seven – Study Pieces

To round off your skills, I've written two full study pieces for you to get your teeth into. They showcase all the ideas you've learned in musically satisfying compositions. They also demonstrate how scales can serve as the foundation of melody, and how playing them in the ways we've explored can raise them far beyond static exercises.

First is a piece I've called *Horsetail Fall*, named after a beautiful waterfall in Yosemite National Park. The name felt fitting for a piece with cascades at its core.

As always, start by learning the piece without adding any expressive elements. This will create a strong mechanical foundation for you to build on as you bring the music to life.

Study Piece Breakdown: Horsetail Fall

Intro (line 1)

This A Major piece opens gently at a *mezzo piano* dynamic and should be played *dolce*. The repeated melody featuring cascading elements should flow smoothly, aided by pull-offs. The line ends with a short, one-bar *crescendo* that's supported by the bass notes and leads into the main theme.

Main Theme (lines 2 & 3)

Shift your picking hand to the *naturale* region over the sound hole. The *crescendo* from the intro leads into a *mezzo forte* dynamic, which continues throughout. The cascading melodies from the introduction are expanded and enriched with bass notes played every two beats, and the open strings allow for smooth position changes. The section is repeated, which gives you the opportunity to experiment with expressive variations.

B Section (lines 4 & 5)

Natural harmonics in A Major are played *mezzo piano* and it will take time to familiarise your fretting hand with the movements between the 5th, 7th, and 12th frets. The section also features short melodies from the scale, incorporating slides and pull-offs to maintain smoothness.

C Section (line 6)

This contrasting section builds melodic movement using the transpositional shapes. Play the entire section with your thumb using rest stroke and begin by dragging your thumb across the sixth and fifth strings. To add contrast, play this section *ponticello*. A long *crescendo* adds excitement and prepares for the triumphant return of a developed main theme.

Main Theme Variation (lines 7 & 8)

The main theme returns here with added variations to further enrich it. Extra melody and bass notes create a fuller texture, all played at a *forte* dynamic following the *crescendo* from the previous section. You can switch back to free stroke and return your picking hand to the *naturale* region. As this section repeats, take advantage of the opportunity to experiment with expressive elements.

Outro (line 9)

The outro revisits ideas from the intro and serves as a bookend to conclude the piece. Shift your picking hand back to the *dolce* region to achieve a sweeter tone. A two-bar *diminuendo* guides the piece to its gentle conclusion as it ends on a *mezzo piano* A Major chord.

Example 7a: Horsetail Fall

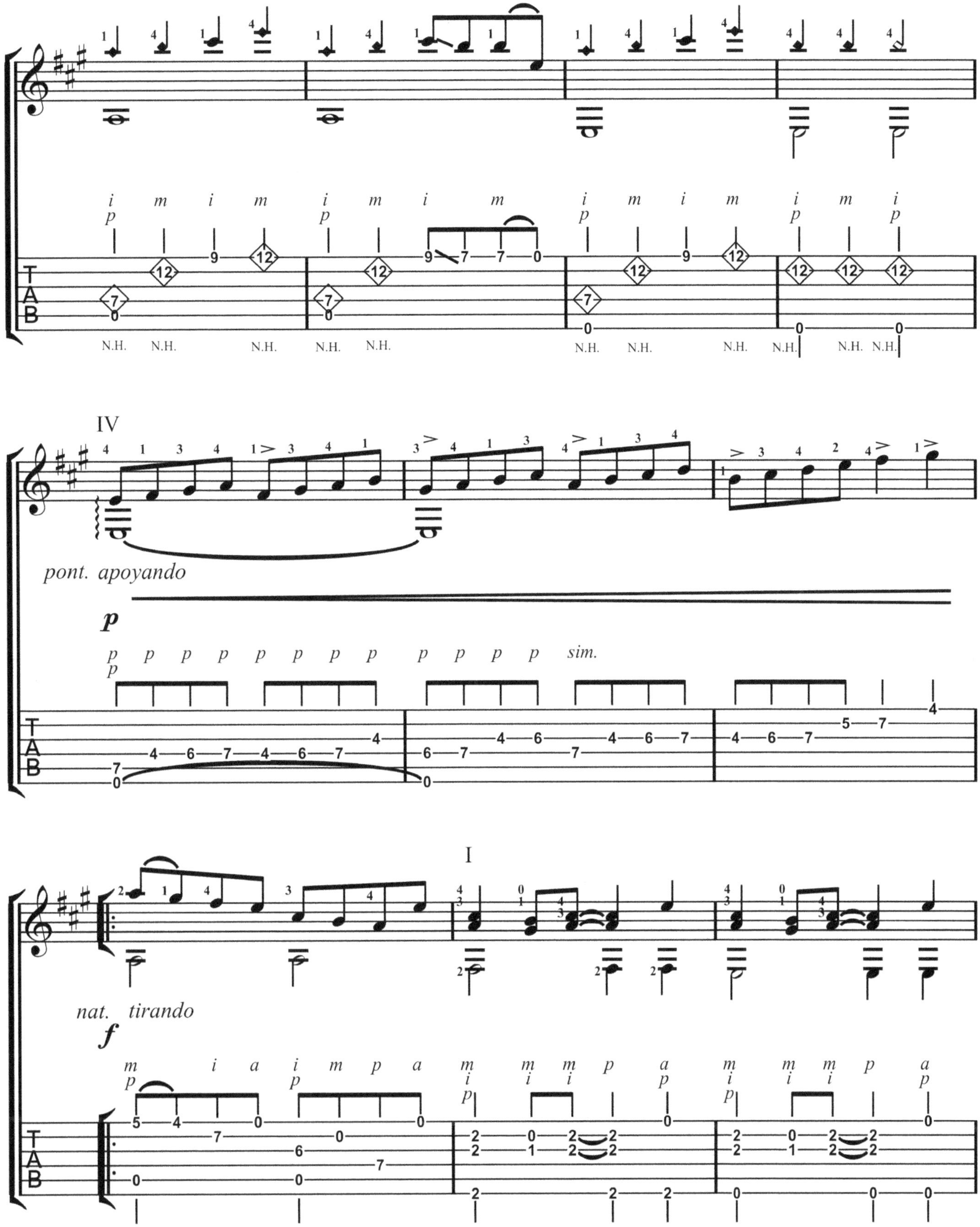
N.H.
IV
pont. apoyando
sim.
I
nat. tirando

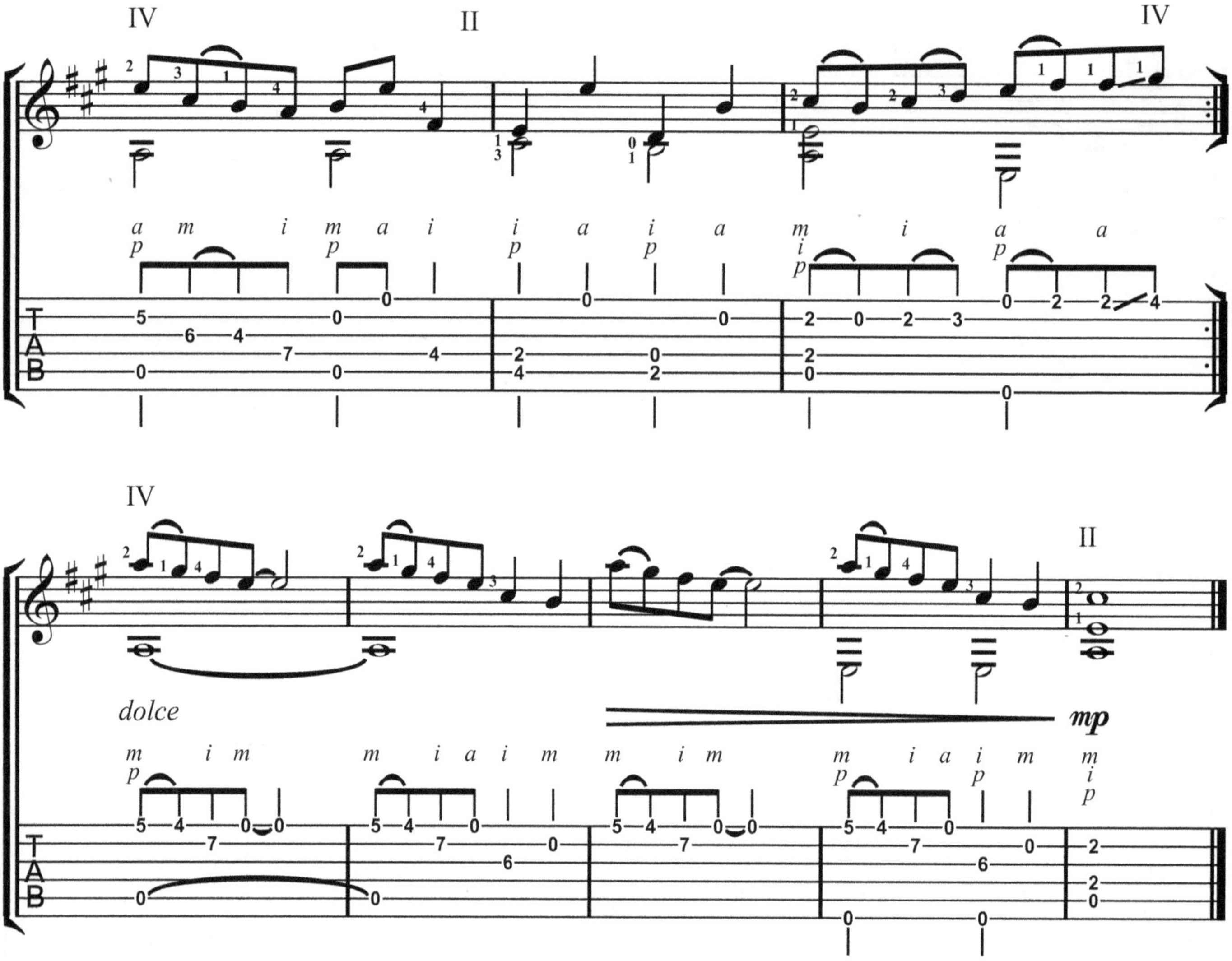
IV
II
IV
IV
II
dolce
mp

Study Piece Breakdown: Moonlight

Intro (line 1)

This waltz in E Minor begins with a simple introduction, presenting the 3/4 rhythm using open string 1/4 notes. It includes natural harmonics from the E Minor scale which should be played *mezzo-forte* and *ponticello* with your picking hand near the bridge.

Main Theme (lines 2 & 3)

E Minor cascades are combined with hammer-ons, slides, and chords that emphasise the waltz rhythm. Use the open strings to help smooth out your transitions between the various fretting hand positions. Play this section with your picking hand around the sound hole in the *naturale* region.

In the final bar of line two, notice the *staccato* accents, which are only written in the notation (not the TAB). Line three introduces another *staccato* moment in the second-time bar and concludes with a *crescendo*, which builds anticipation for the next section.

B Section (lines 4 & 5)

This section begins *forte* on the first beat before dropping to *mezzo piano*. The opening notes sustain as a more delicate E Minor theme unfolds. Interpret this section softly and sweetly with your picking hand shifted to *dolce*.

Be mindful of *staccato* markings on beat 2 in some bars, and ensure that the accompanying open-string harmonies sustain without being accidentally muted. The section concludes with a short melodic phrase and a *crescendo* leading to the bridge.

Bridge (line 6)

The bridge continues the melody and *crescendo* heard at the end of the B section and leads to a variation of the ideas heard in the intro played *forte*. The natural harmonics at the end of the bridge lead you to the *D.S. al Coda*, where you repeat the main theme.

D.S al Coda (lines 2, 3 & 4)

The *Dal Segno* instructs you to return to the second line (marked by the *segno* symbol), for another repeat of the main theme. Use this repeat to vary some of the expressive elements. The *To Coda* direction at the end of line four takes you to the Coda.

Coda (lines 7 & 8)

The Coda expands on ideas from the B Section and introduces new chord voicings in open position. During these two lines, gradually move your picking hand from *dolce* to *ponticello*. Maintaining control of your picking hand while keeping relaxed is the key to playing this section musically.

Outro (lines 9 & 10)

The outro brings the piece to a conclusion with some delicately played *harp* and *artificial harmonics*. Spend time finding and articulating the artificial harmonic elements before gradually integrating the other notes to create the harp-like phrases. Play the entire outro delicately with a *piano* dynamic.

And there you have it, *Moonlight*! Enjoy exploring how the various types of scales come together in this piece, and feel free to make it your own by experimenting with the expressive elements.

Example 7b: Moonlight

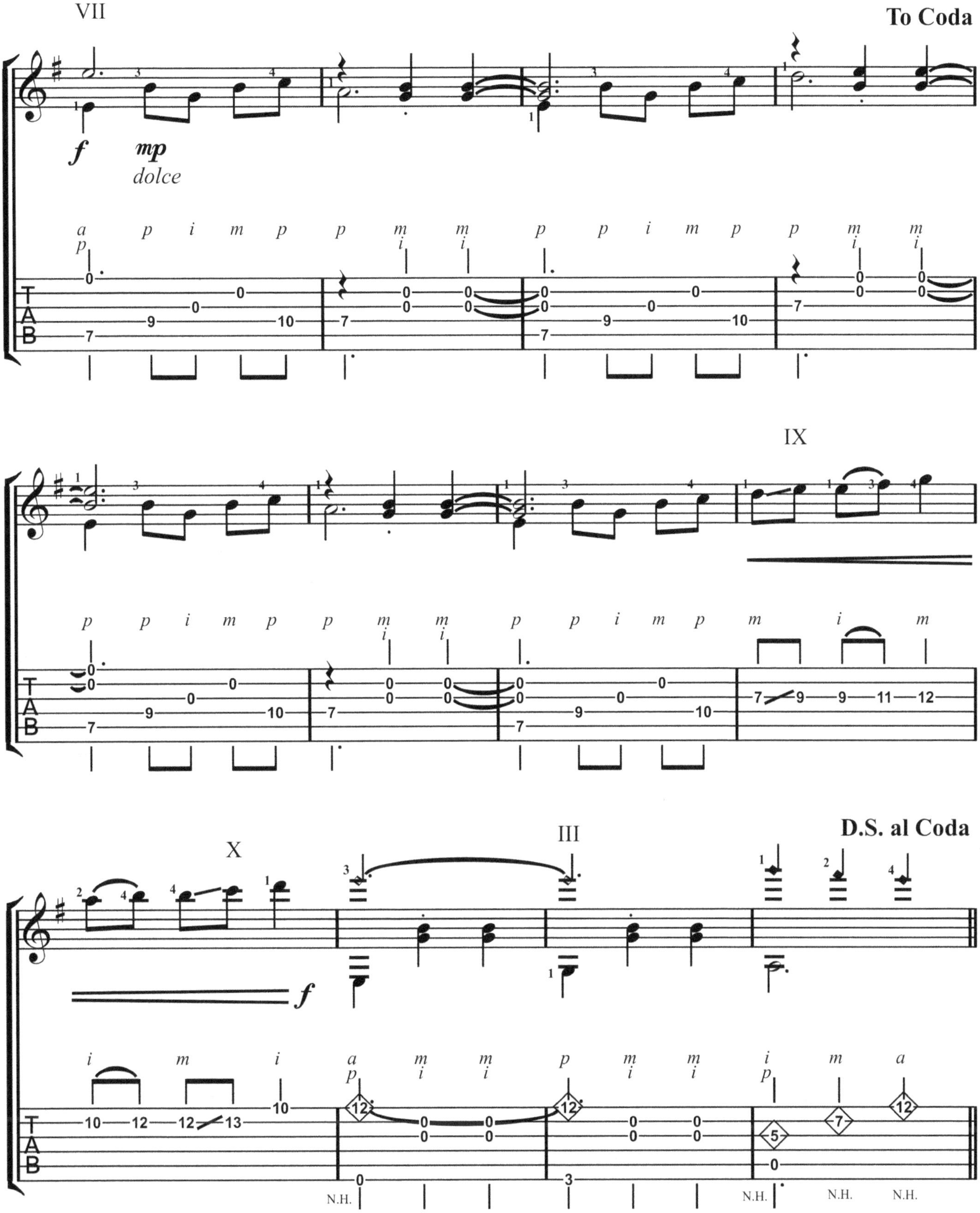
VII
To Coda
f
mp
dolce
IX
X
III
D.S. al Coda
N.H.

dolce
a p i m p p m i m i p p i m p p m i m i
pont.
p p i m p p m i m i p p i m p p
p
A.H.14 A.H.12 A.H.16 A.H.14 A.H.12 A.H.12 A.H.14 A.H.12 A.H.16 A.H.14 A.H.12 A.H.12
A.H.14 A.H.12 A.H.16 A.H.14 A.H.12 A.H.12 A.H.14 A.H.12 A.H.16 A.H.14 A.H.12

Conclusion

The goal of this book has been to give you a fresh perspective on scales, with a strong focus on musicality and expression. You should now see that scales can offer so much more than linear movements through the notes of a key, and I hope you've enjoyed this unique approach to exploring their potential. I hope practicing the material here has given you the foundation to take these ideas further and make them your own.

The skills you've learned will quickly become a natural part of your playing if you're mindful about exploring them. Whether you're interested in composing on the guitar or refining your technique while deepening your understanding of the fretboard, everything we've discussed here can support your unique musical journey.

I encourage you to take these concepts and personalise them. Try to compose pieces inspired by them and learn new scales in a more musically engaged way. Ultimately, try to use this knowledge to enrich your learning of new repertoire. Above all, let these ideas help make your playing more expressive and enjoyable.

Scales are wonderful tools, and when approached in a way that goes beyond playing notes in succession, they can become an exciting and rewarding part of your guitar journey.

I wish you all the best in your practice and remind you that any time spent with a guitar in your hands is time well spent.

Will McNicol

Bonus Chapter: More Cascading Scales

Just before we wrap up, I wanted to share a bonus chapter for you to dig into. At the start of this book we explored cascading scales in the keys of E Major, E Minor, A Major, and A Minor. While they are also fantastic to explore in other keys, their nature can make it time-consuming to discover them at first. To help you on your way, I'm giving you this collection of cascading scales in several other keys.

In this chapter, you'll learn one-octave cascading scales in the following keys:

- C Major & C Minor

- D Major & D Minor

- G Major & G Minor

- F Major & F Minor

- B Major & B Minor

Some of these scales involve larger stretches for your fretting hand or the occasional half-barre to allow the notes to blend. Here are a few tips to keep in mind as you work through them:

- **Adjust your fretting-hand thumb position:** Placing it toward the middle of the neck can increase the reach for your fingers

- **Keep your fingers floating above the frets:** This helps maintain a ready position where your fingers are poised to fret notes efficiently

- **Avoid over-extending your wrist:** Stretching your wrist outward too far can cause tension and discomfort. Instead, focus on keeping your hand relaxed and positioned naturally

We'll start with C Major. This scale involves a stretch between the 3rd and 7th frets, allowing the F and E notes in bars two and three to sustain. If the stretch feels too far, don't worry, you can gradually work up to it.

Example 8a: C Major

76

In C Natural Minor, we see the Bb note blending with Ab in bar one while the open G sustains throughout the next two bars. In bars two and three, pairs of notes sustain and allow Eb, F, and G to harmonise beautifully. The A note in bar four can sustain through the repeat to bar one.

Example 8b: C Minor

With D Major, start in the third position. The open B in bar one allows the shift to fourth position as your fourth finger plays the 7th fret. Stay in the 4th position until bar four, where you move back to the third position and use your fourth finger for C#.

Keep position changes smooth by moving your fretting-hand thumb only once per shift.

Example 8c: D Major

With D Natural Minor, you'll encounter larger stretches between the 3rd and 7th frets, so keep the earlier tips in mind. The first bar sees D blending with C, and Bb blending with A. The first three notes in bar two sustain together, while the E and open D blend into bar three. The C note in bar four sustains through the repeat.

Example 8d: D Minor

G Major features the first G sustaining while F# is played. The open E sustains through bar one and into bar two, where the C can ring until the open G. Bar three includes a sustained fourth-string A. In bar four, changing the fretting finger for D allows the A note to sustain.

Example 8e: G Major

In G Minor, the open E and B strings aren't available, so a half-barre at the 3rd fret allows G, D, and Bb notes to sustain. The "1/2CIII" marking in the music shows where to hold the barre. Release the barre at the end of bar two to let the A and open G notes ring, then reapply it at the end of bar three.

Example 8f: G Minor

F Major uses the open E and G for sustained notes. Stretches here require your fourth finger on the fourth and fifth strings. Bringing your elbow into your body can help position your wrist for these reaches.

Example 8g: F Major

F Minor presents another challenge for cascading scales due to the absence of open E and B strings. Keep your second finger on Eb throughout the scale for sustained harmony. Open G and F notes in the middle bars also ring together. Start with your fretting hand in a position that avoids unnecessary movement.

Example 8h: F Minor

In B Major, we shift from the sixth to fourth position in bar two, then back to sixth position in bar four. An open E creates time for these transitions as the A# sustains into bar two. The third finger suggestion for the open B at the end of bar two may seem unconventional but ensures a smooth transition.

Example 8i: B Major

Finally, B Natural Minor contains position changes helped by the open Es in bars two and three. Your picking-hand choices mirror those in D Major, including the third finger for the open B at the end of bar two.

Example 8j: B Minor

Now take what you've learned here and extend these cascading scales into new octaves, as we did earlier in the book. Exploring scales in this way unlocks the fretboard and offers new, musical approaches to playing guitar.

Have fun!